Fantastic ANIMALS

GRAYSCALE COLORING BOOKS

VOLUME 4.

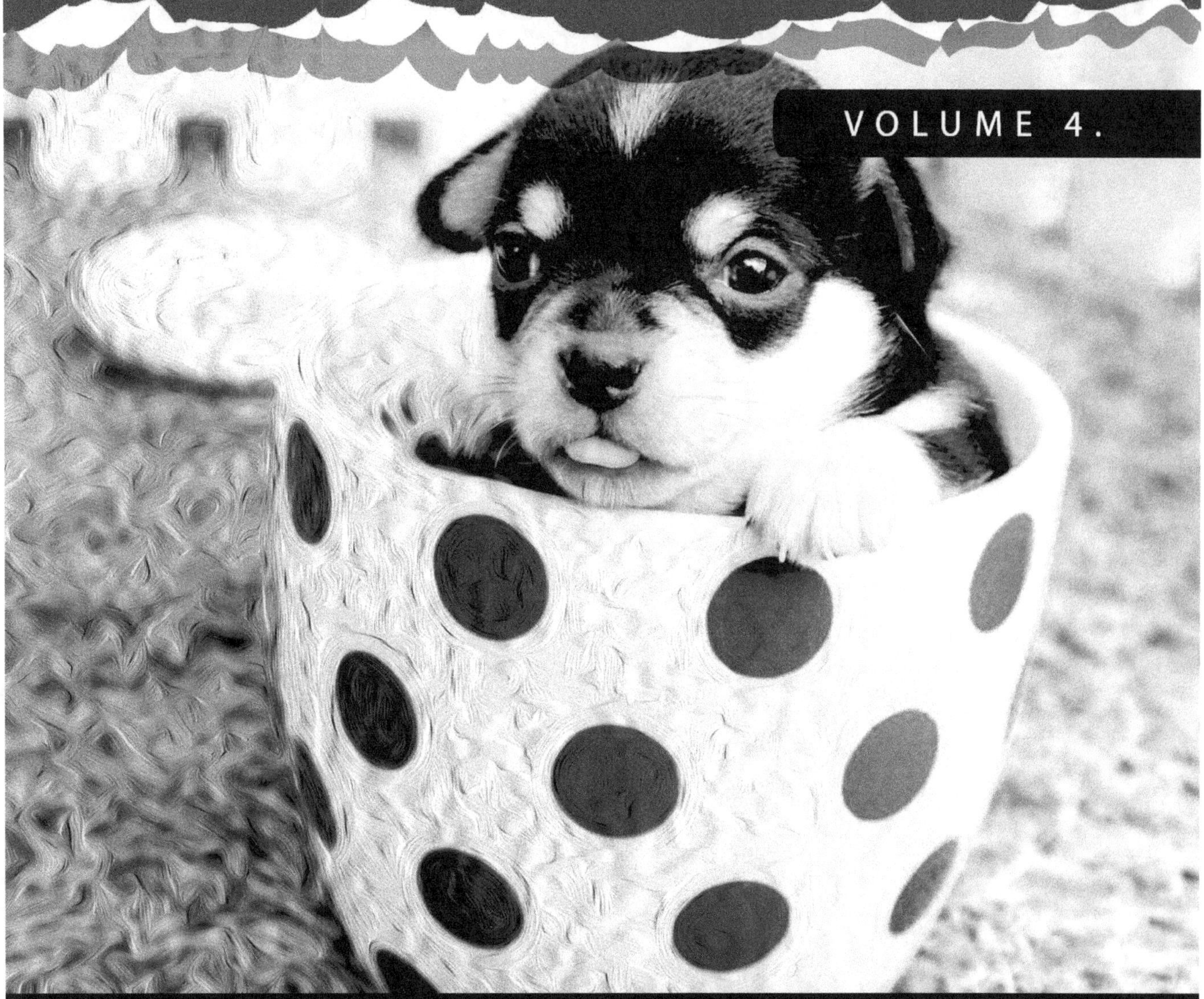

COLOR TEST PAGE

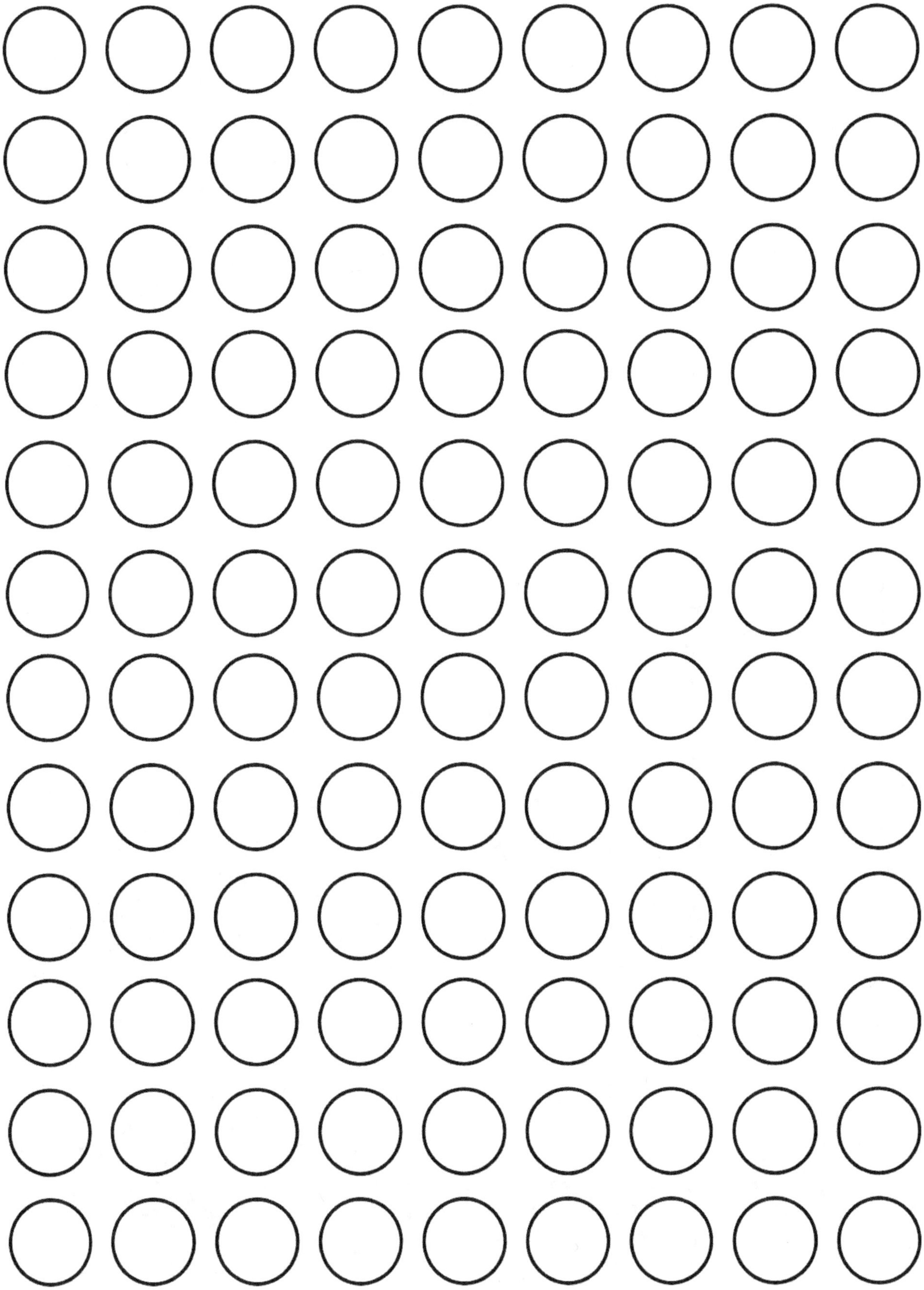

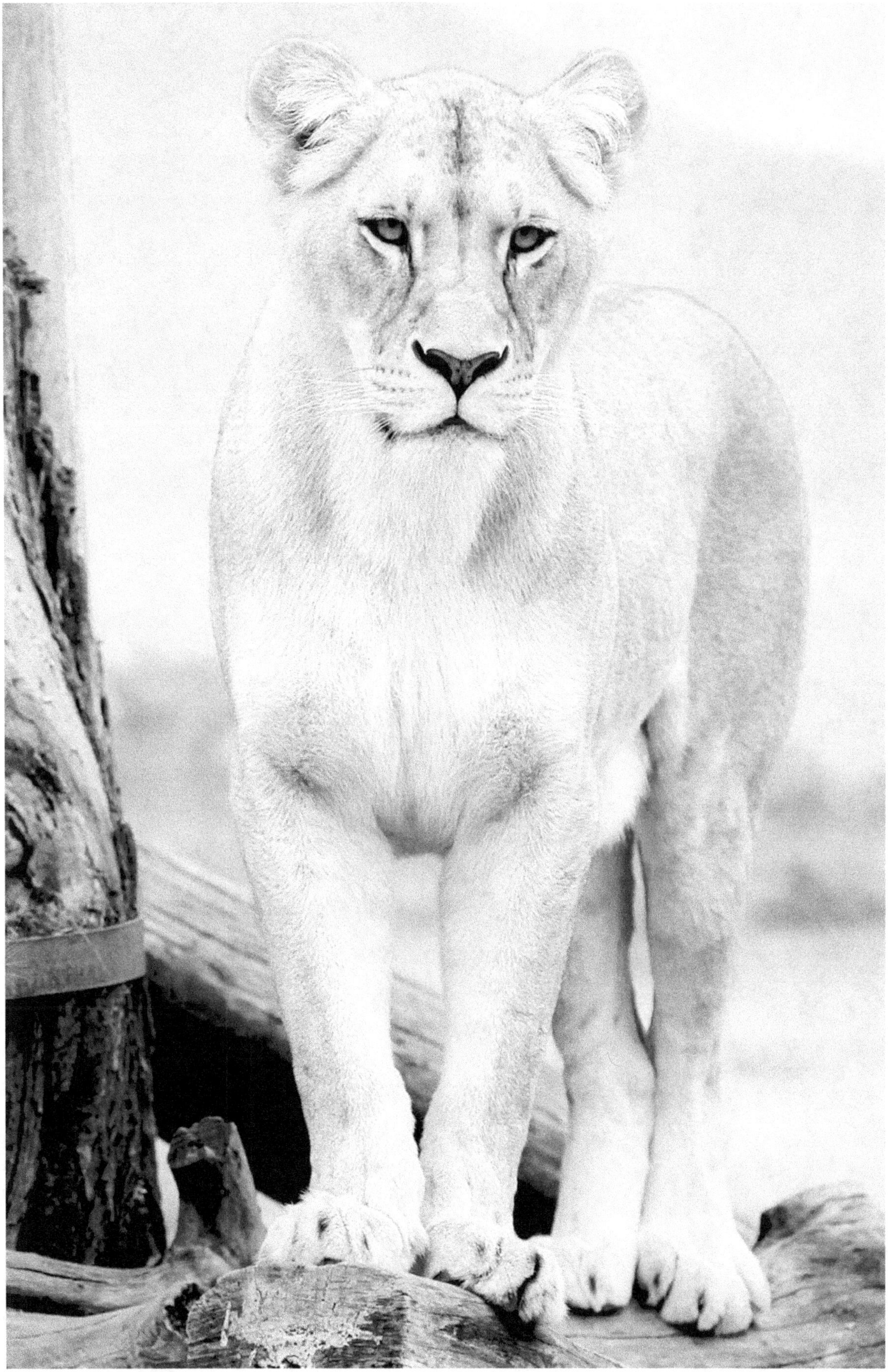

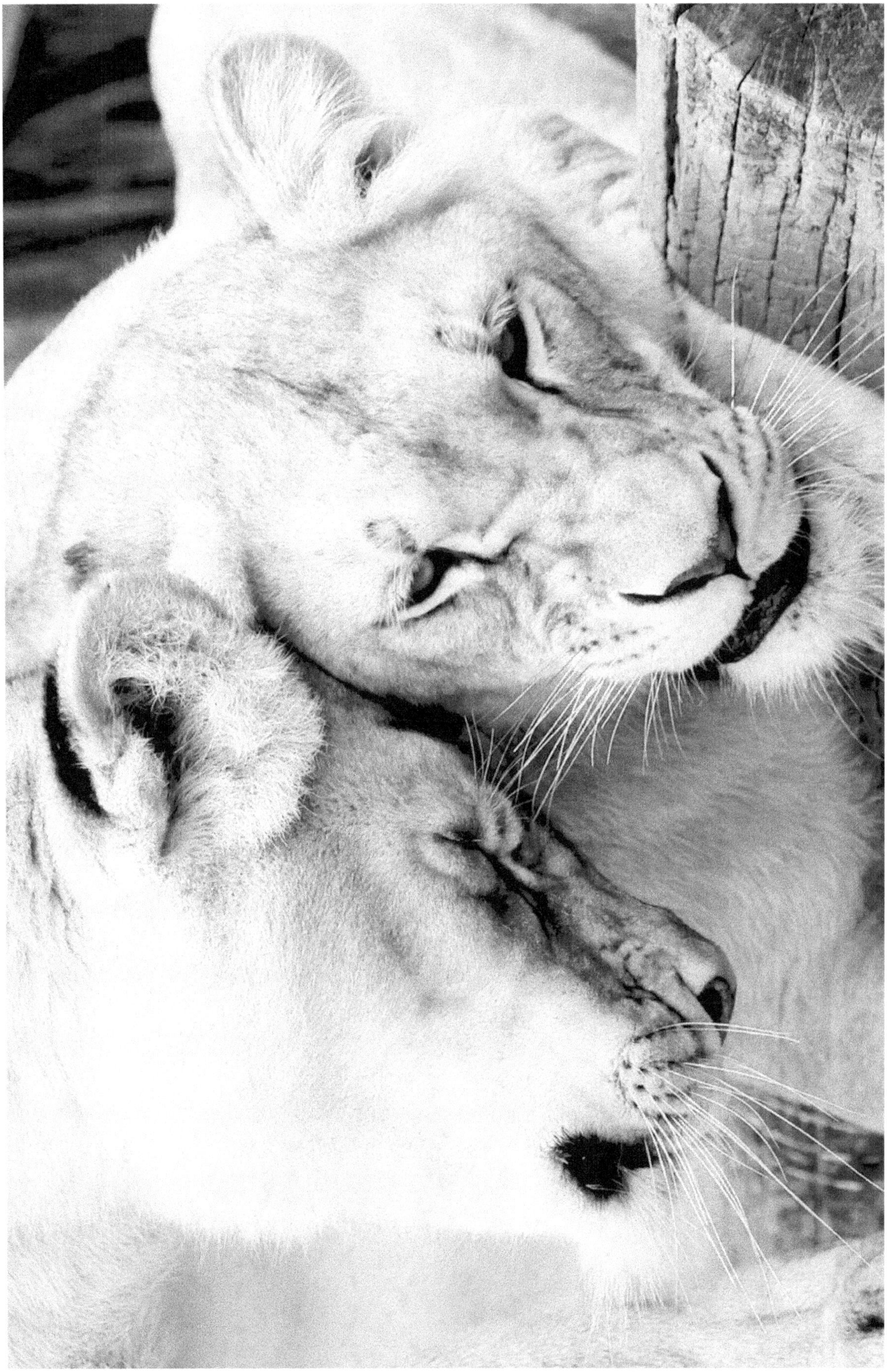

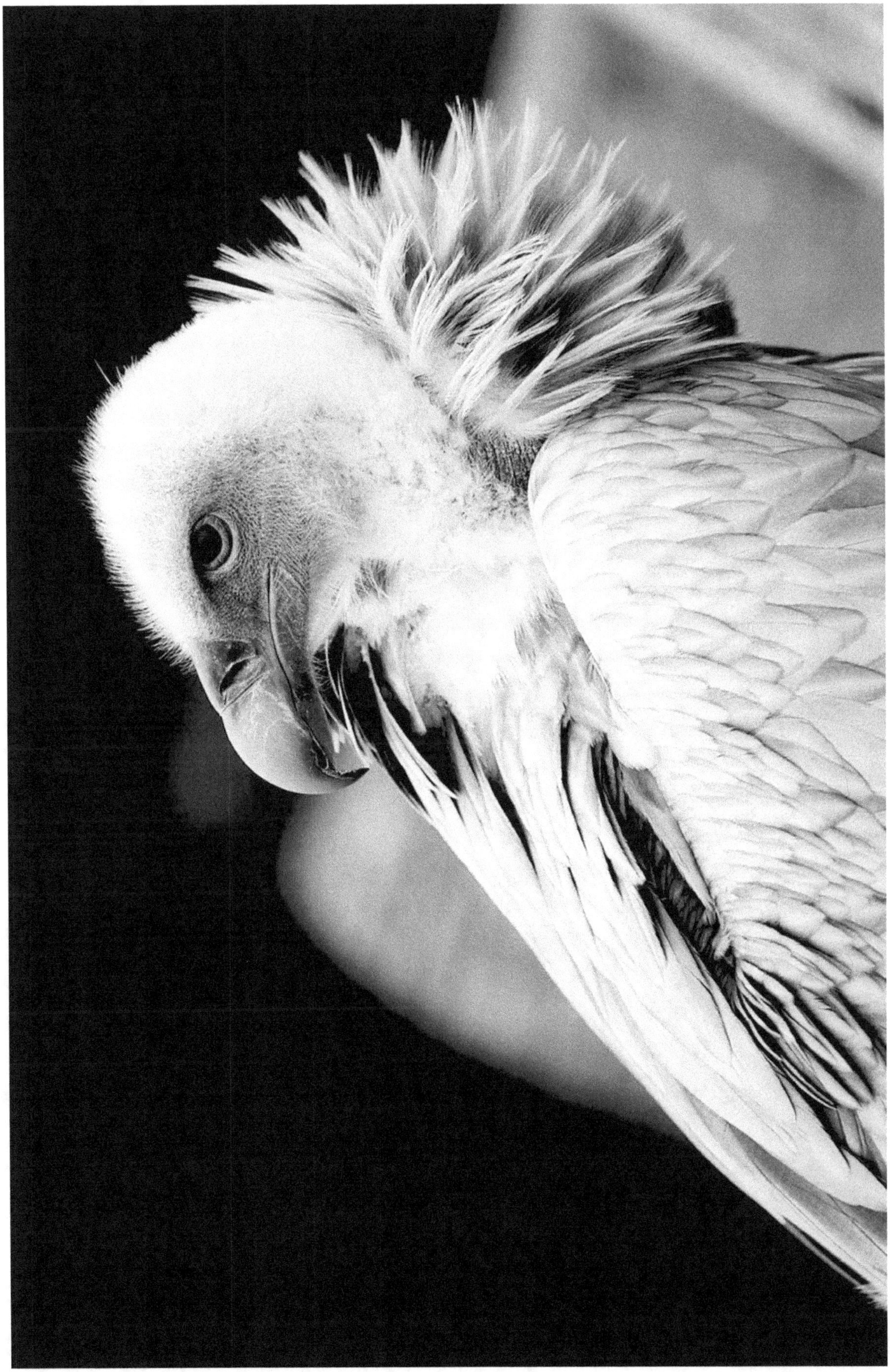

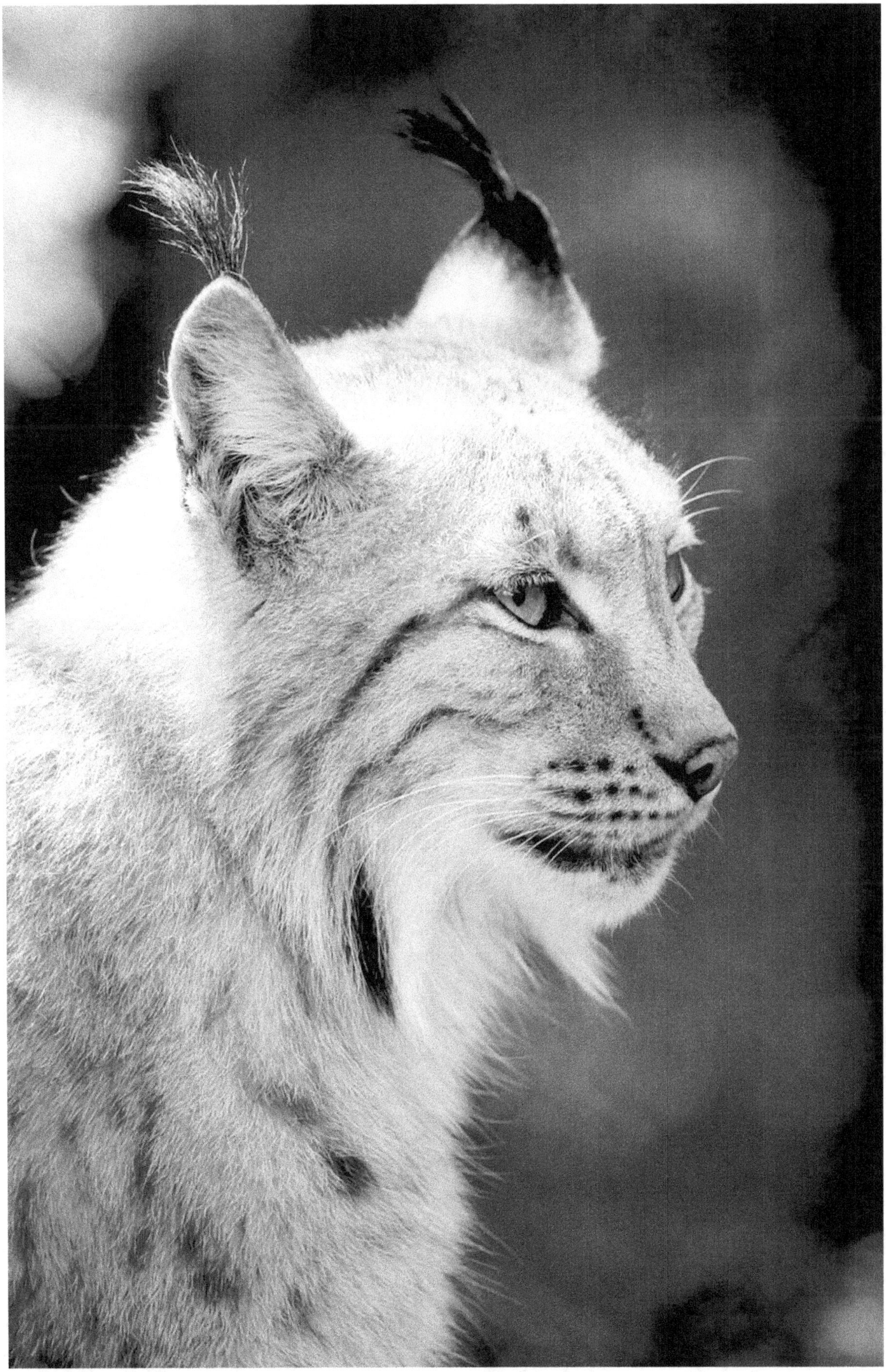

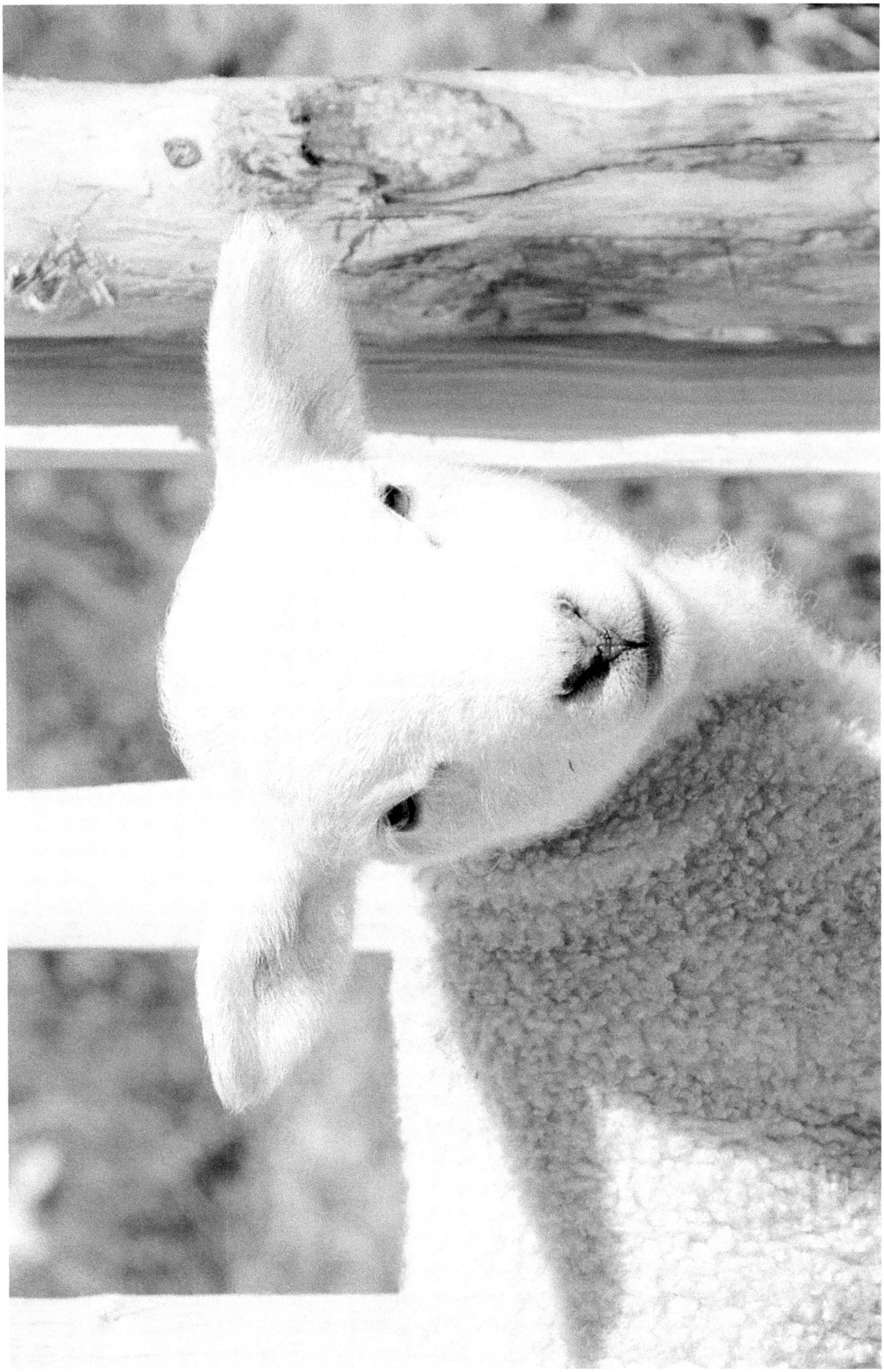

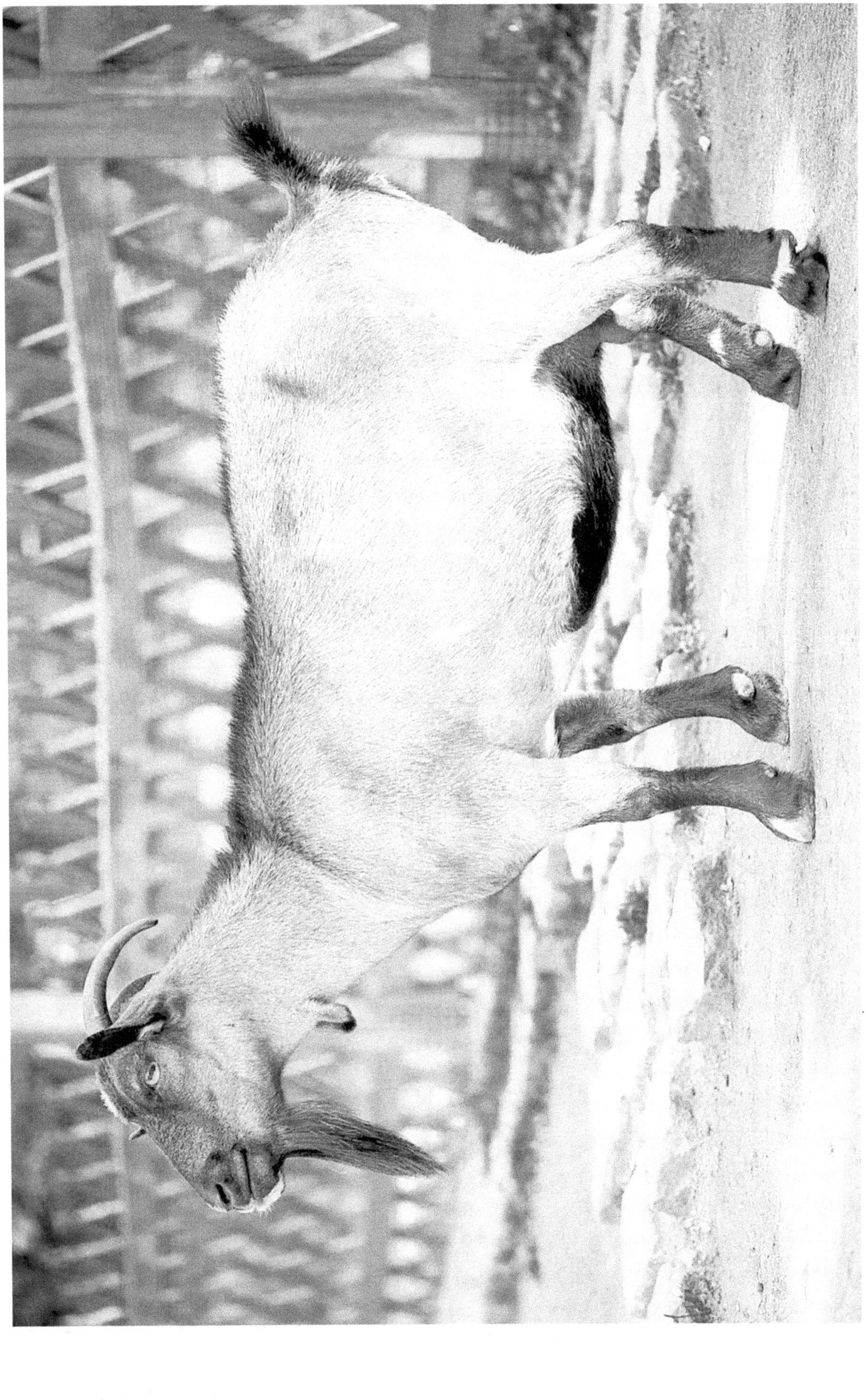

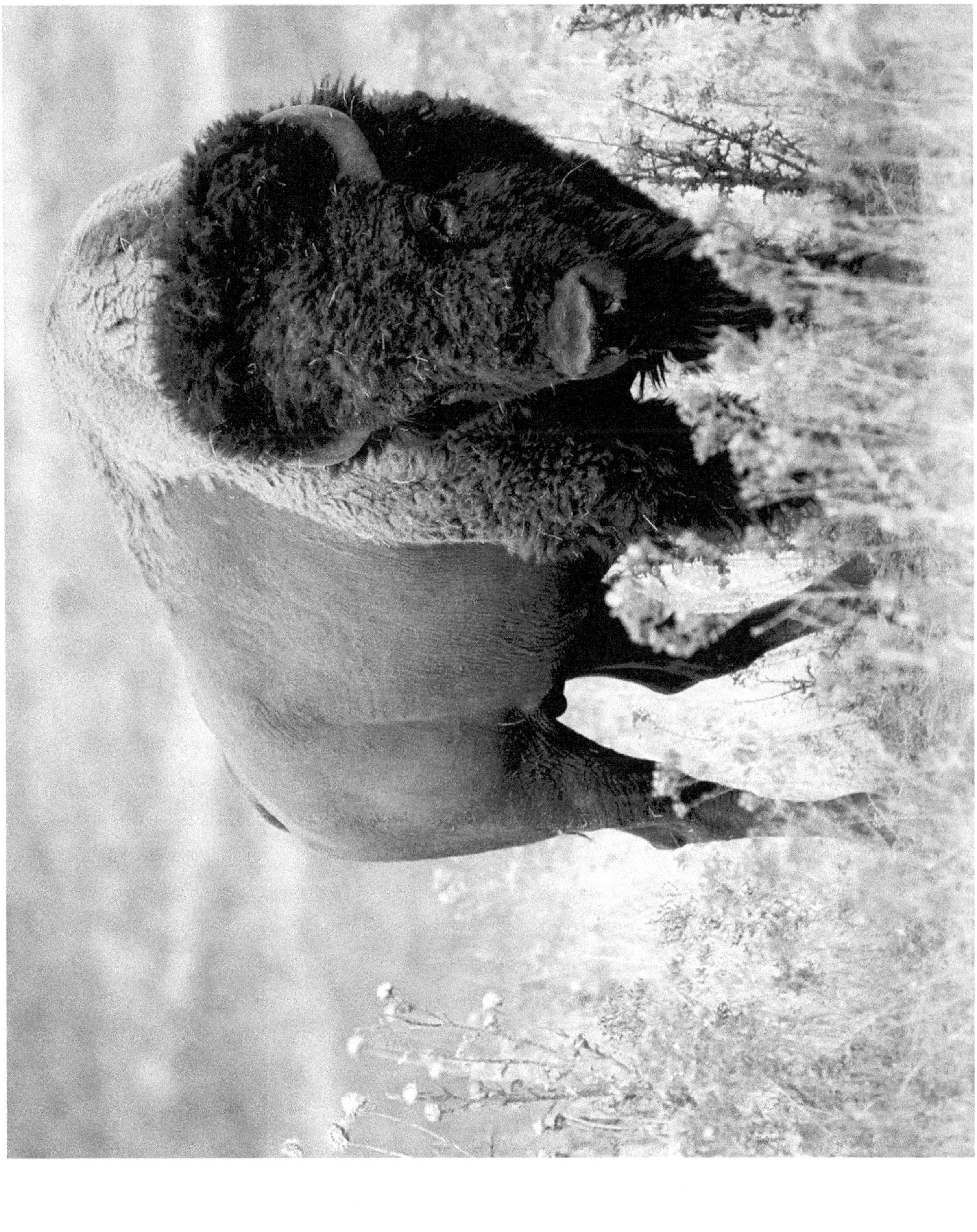

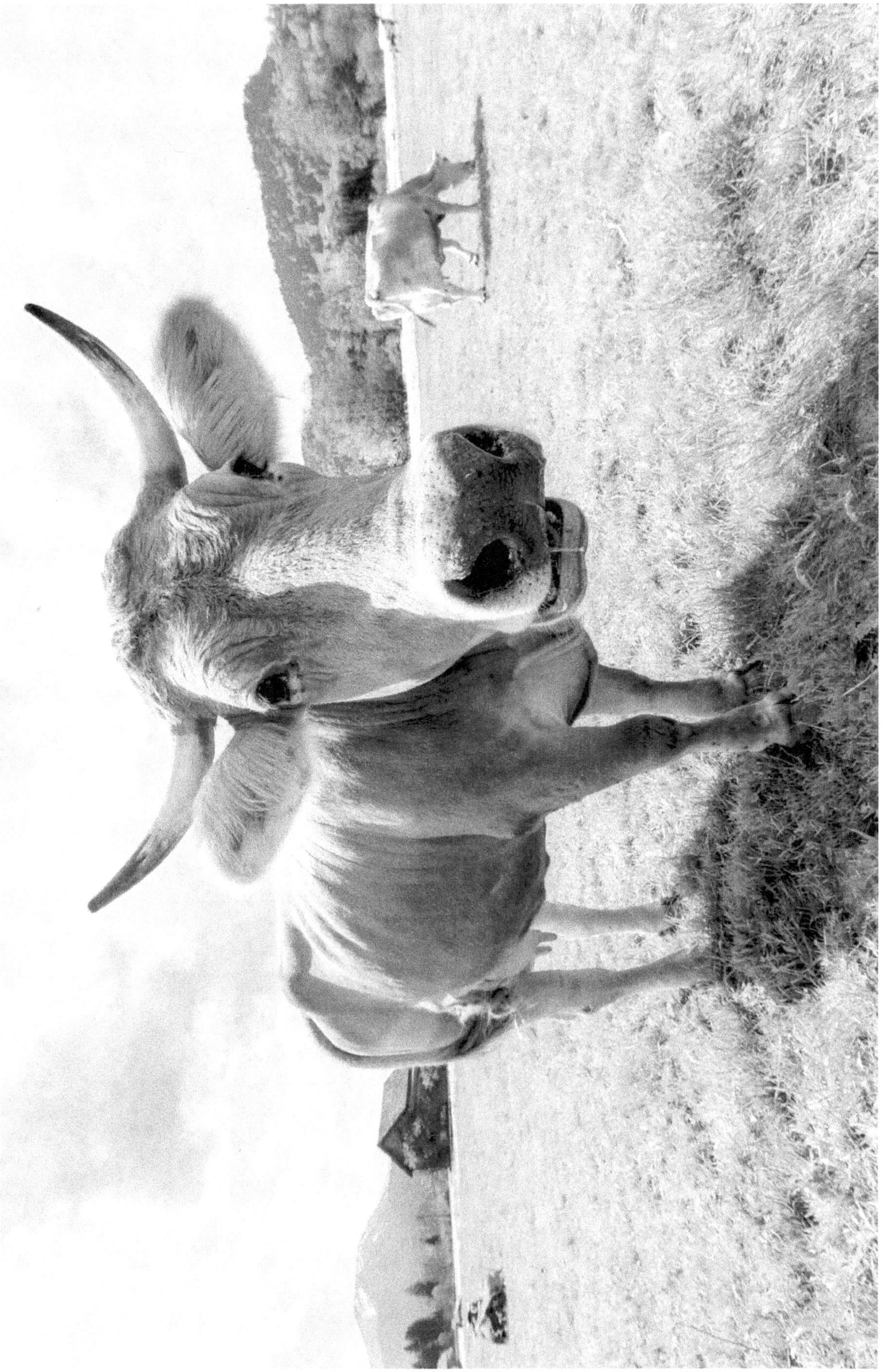

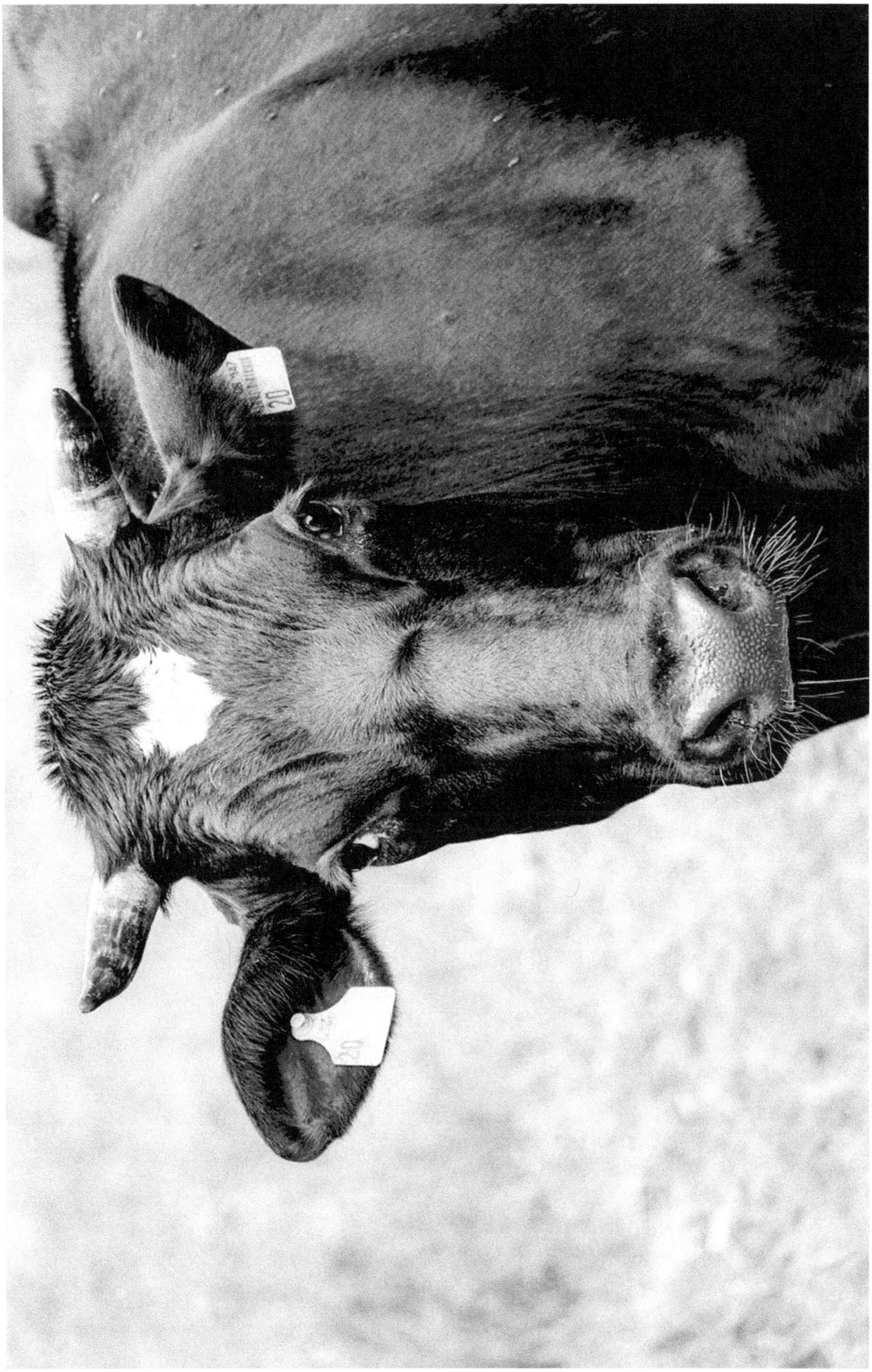
20
20

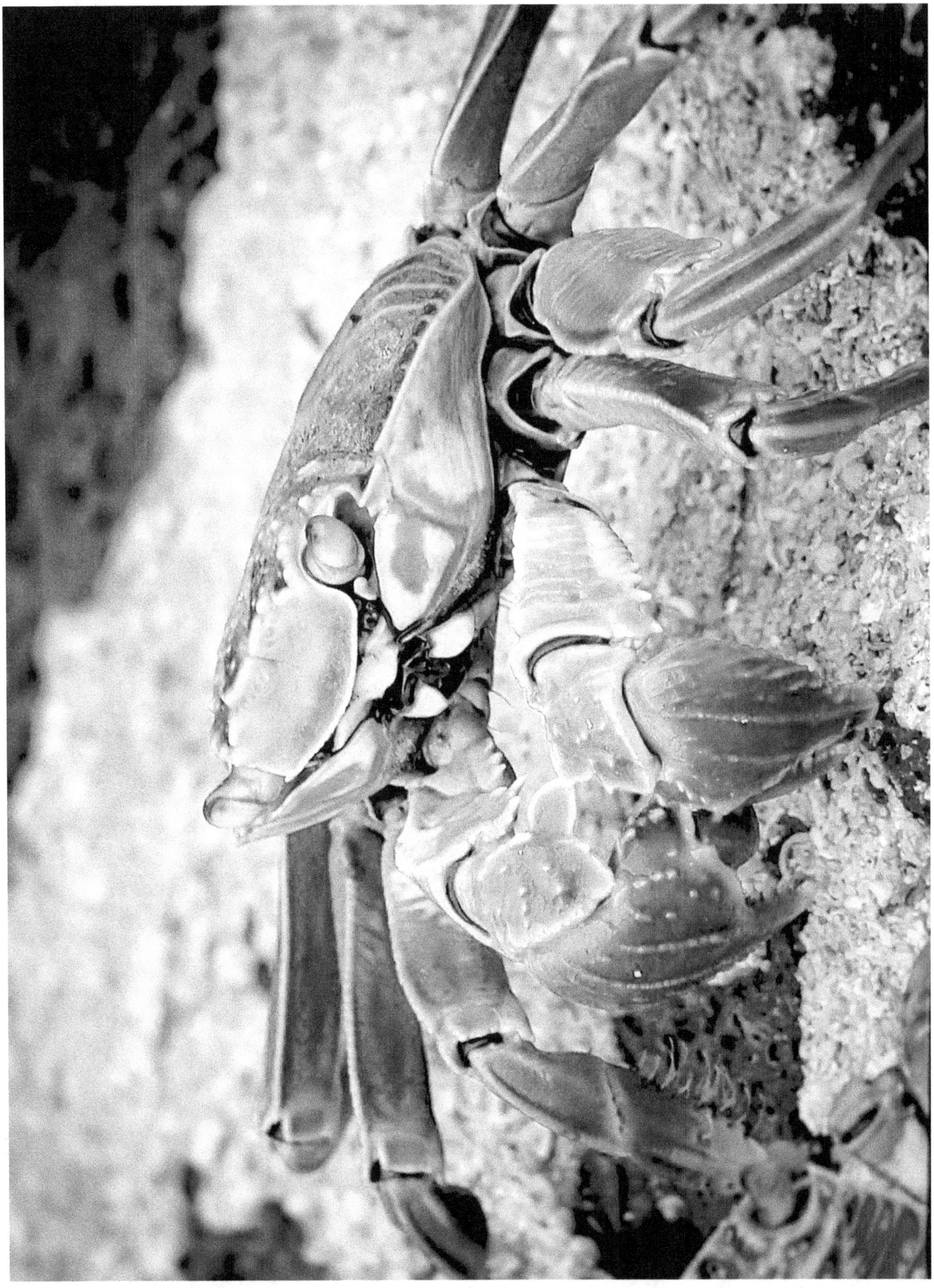

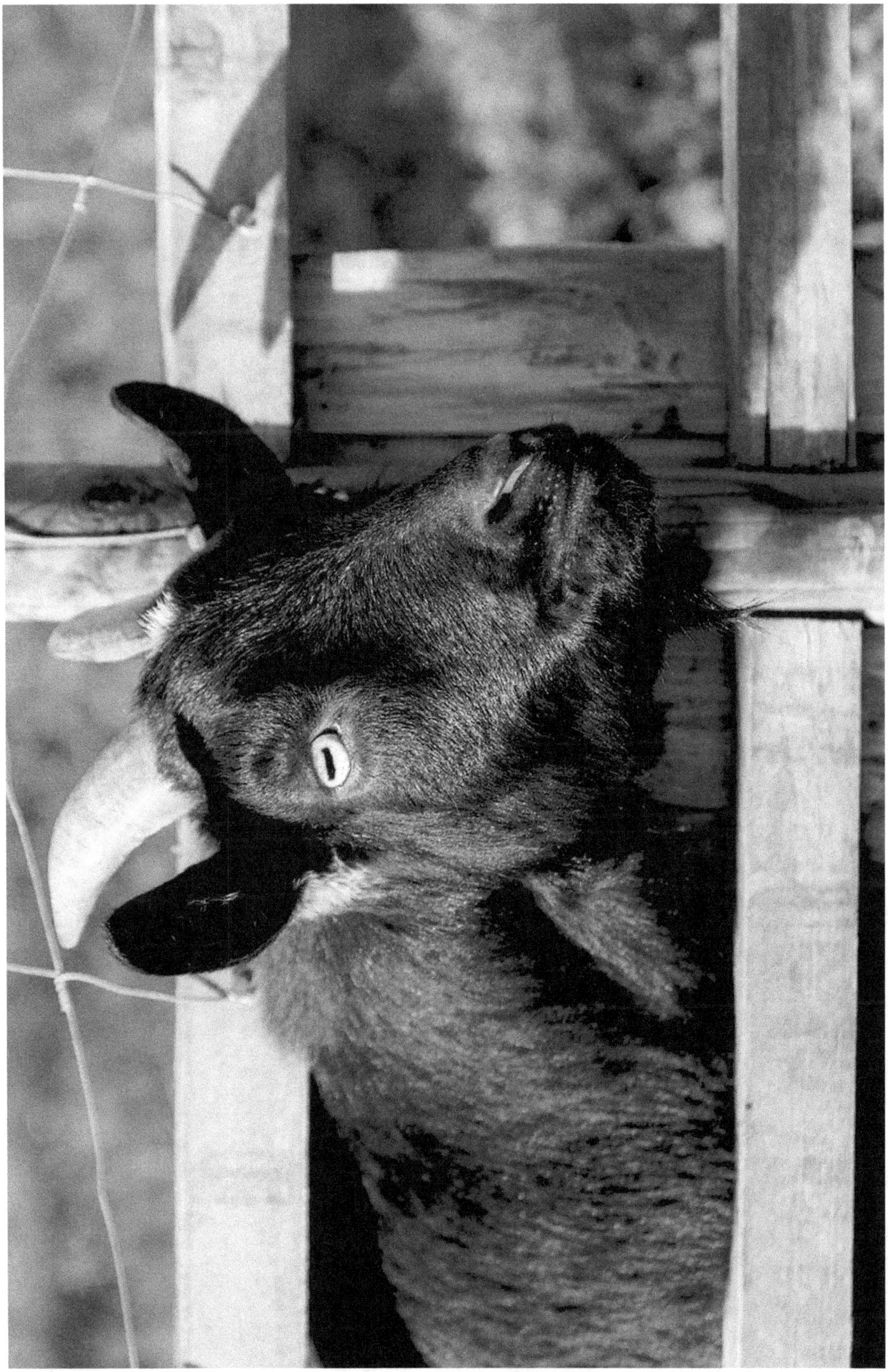

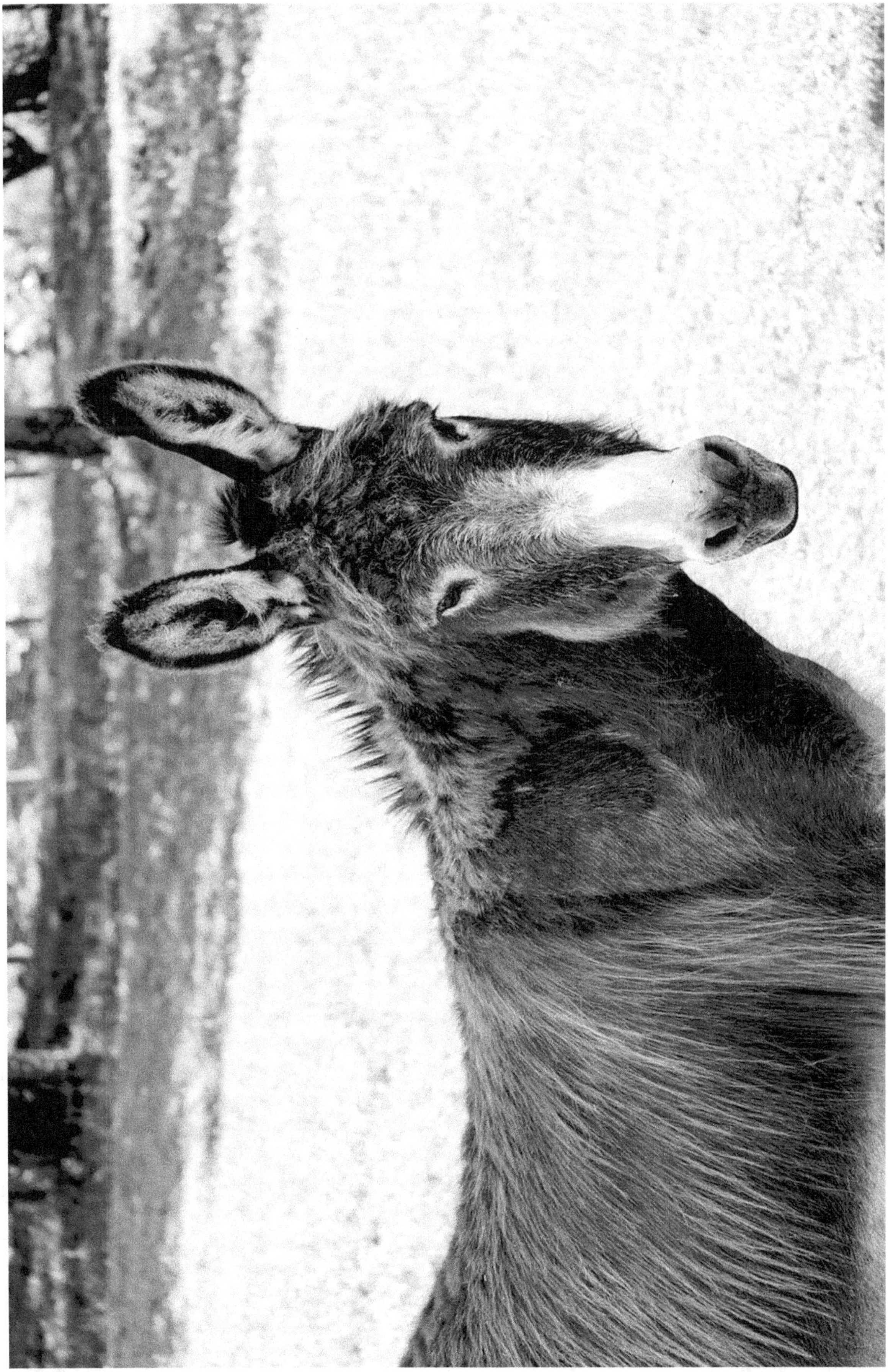

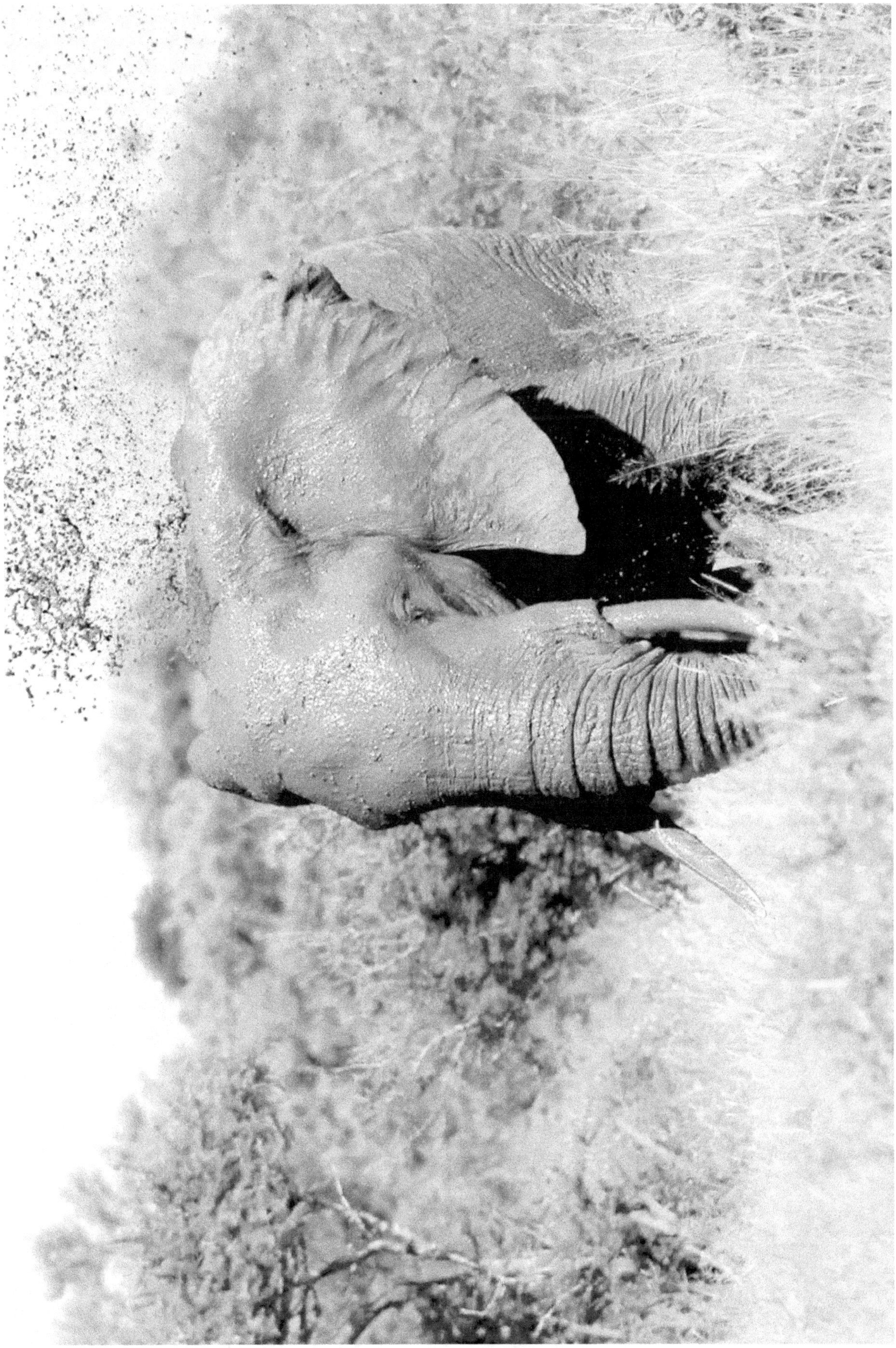

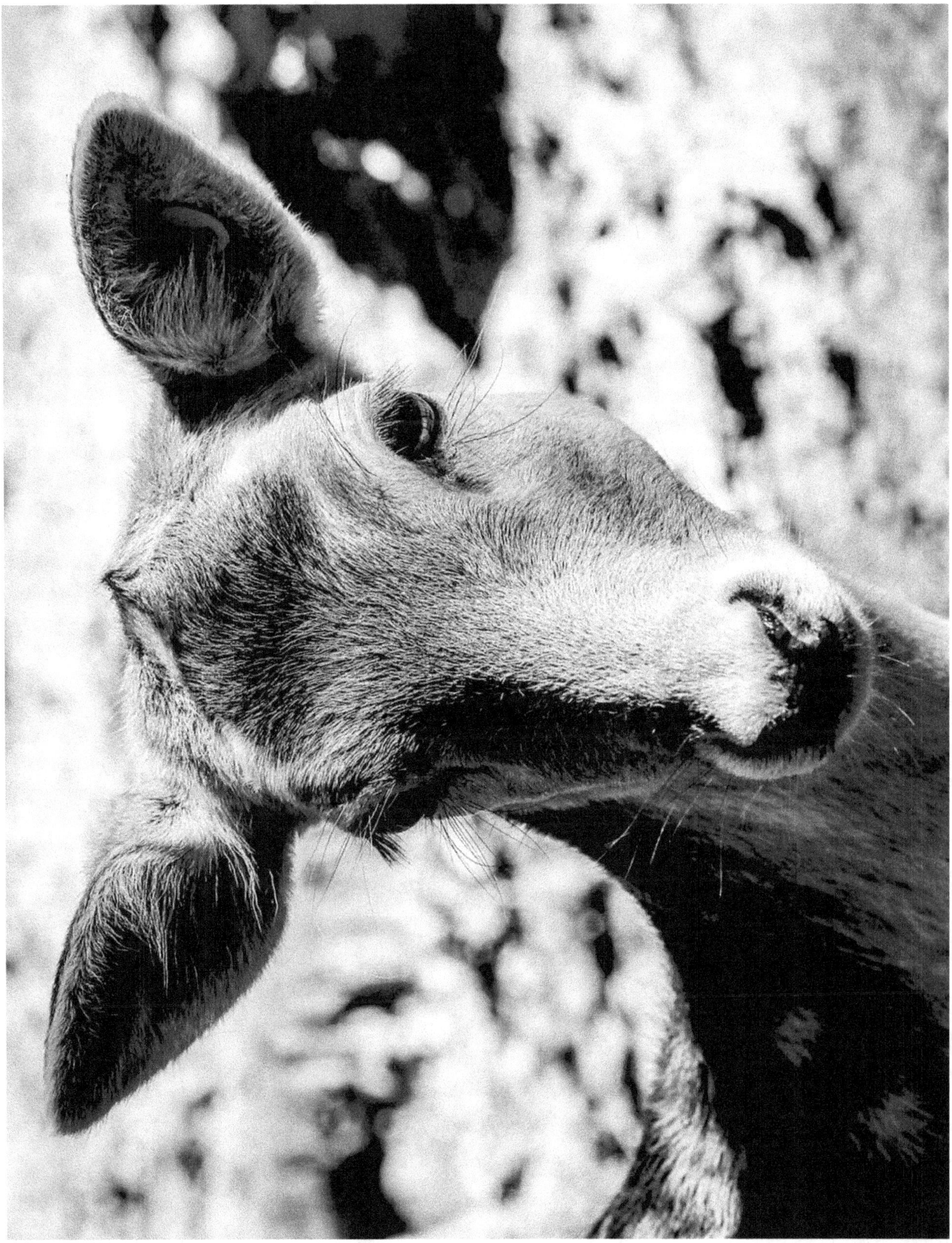

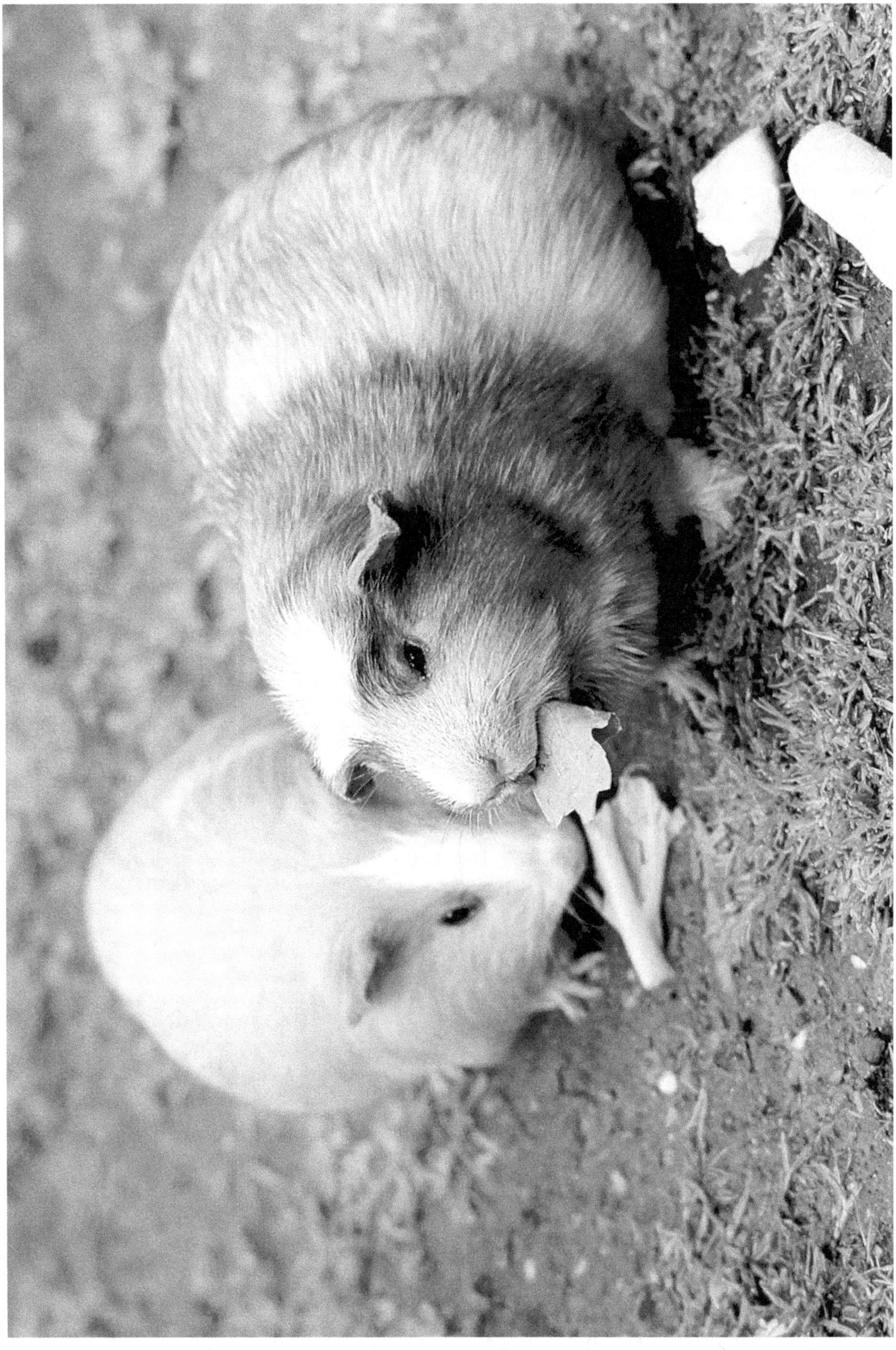

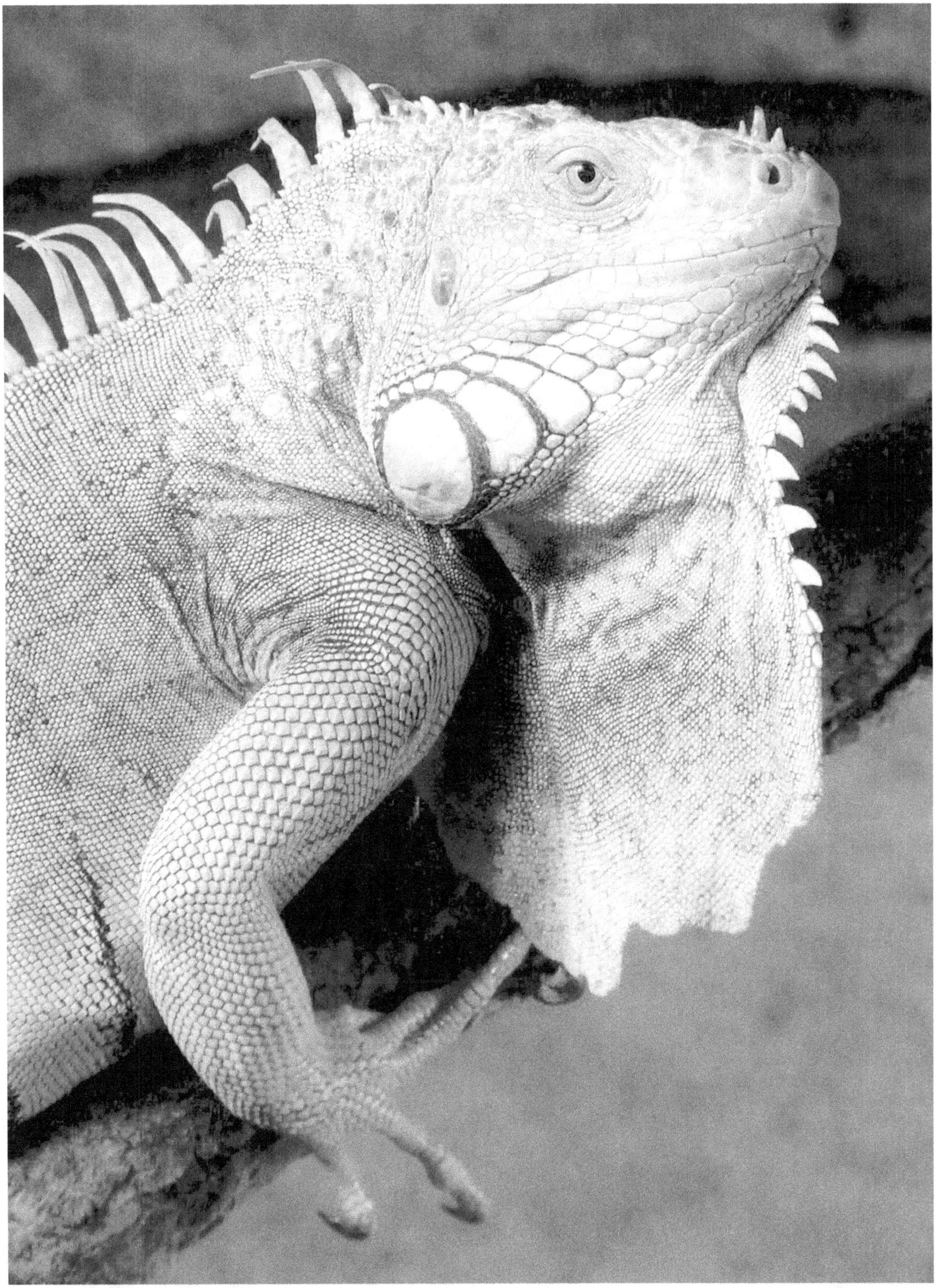

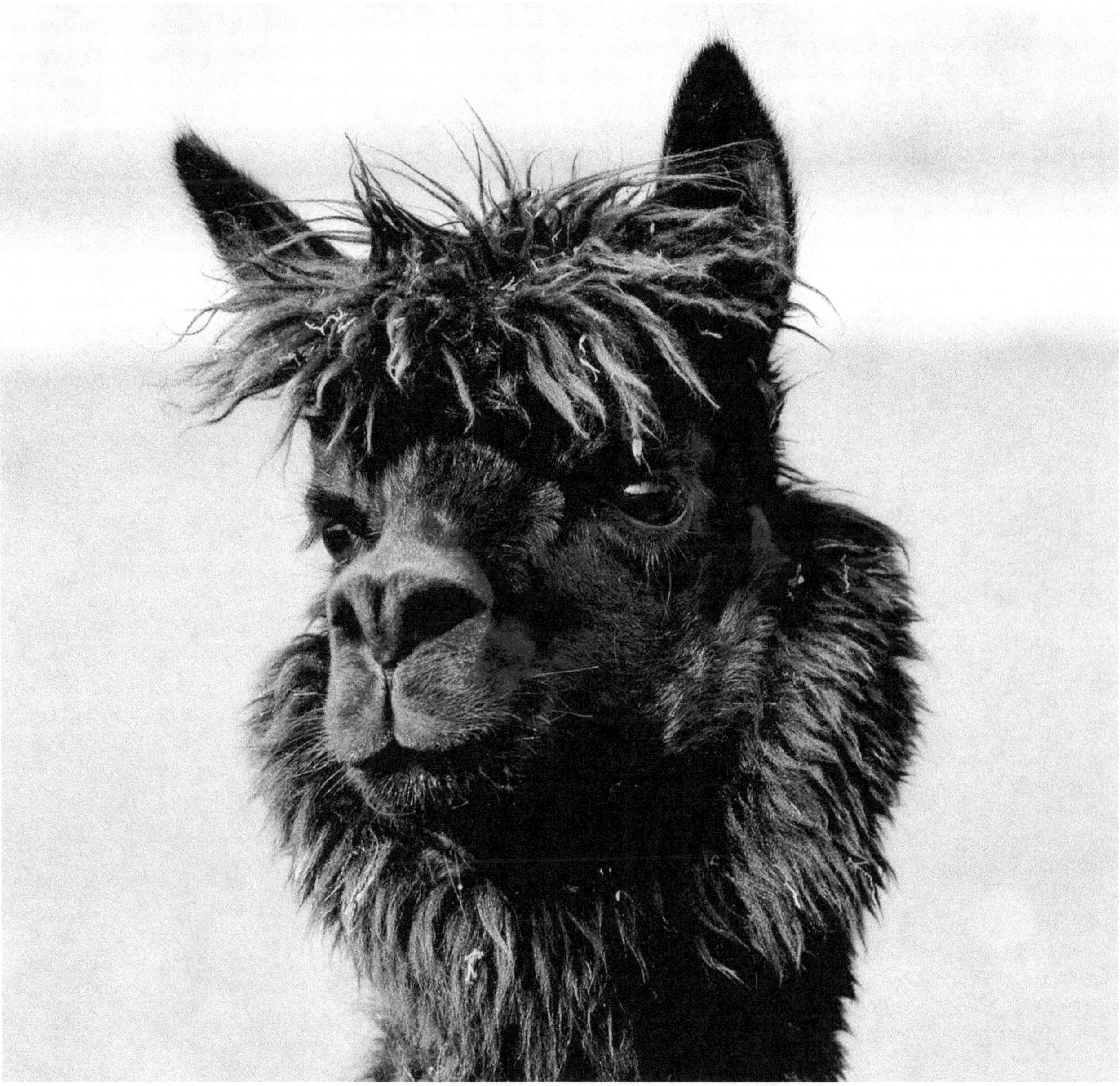

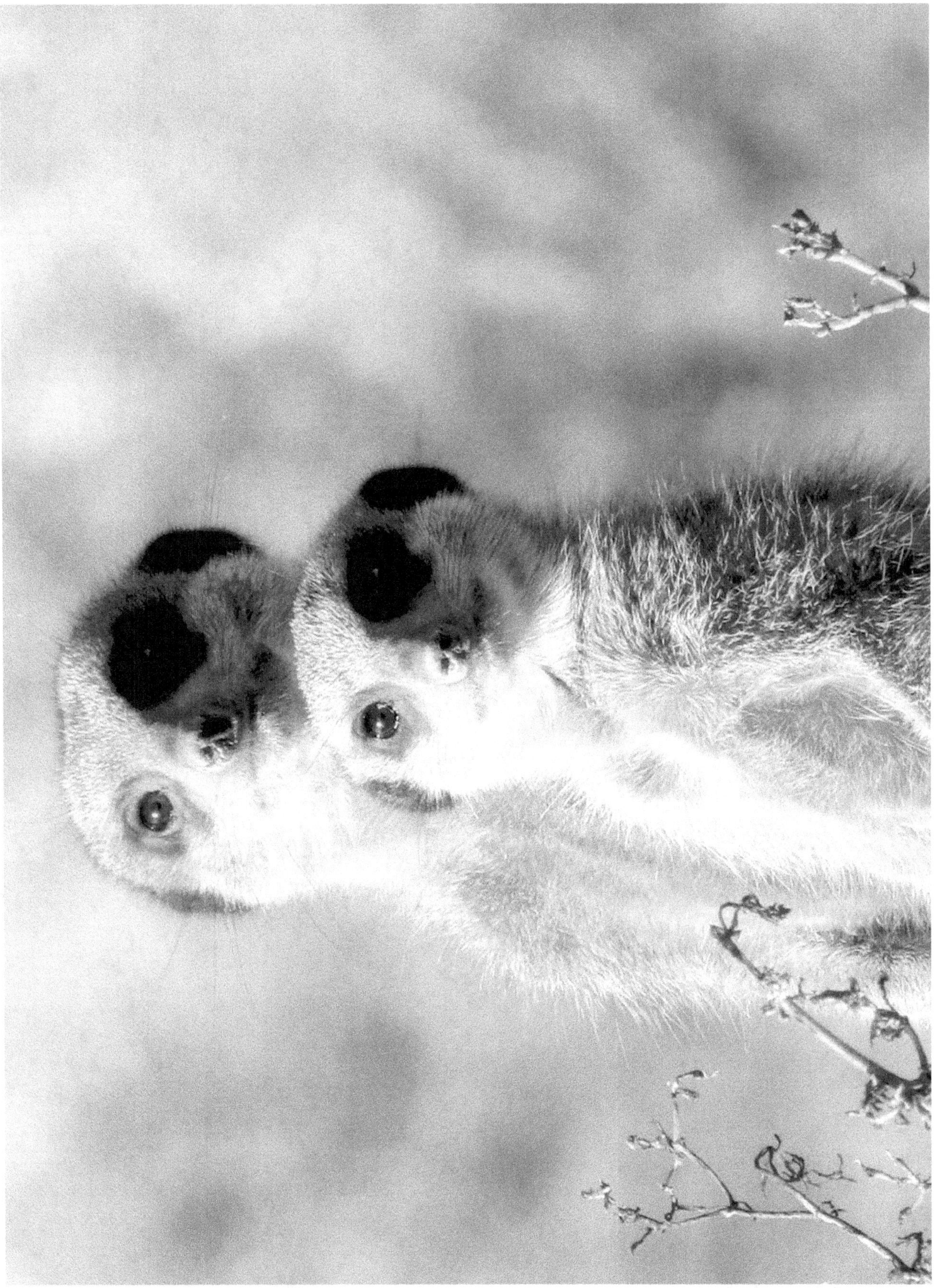

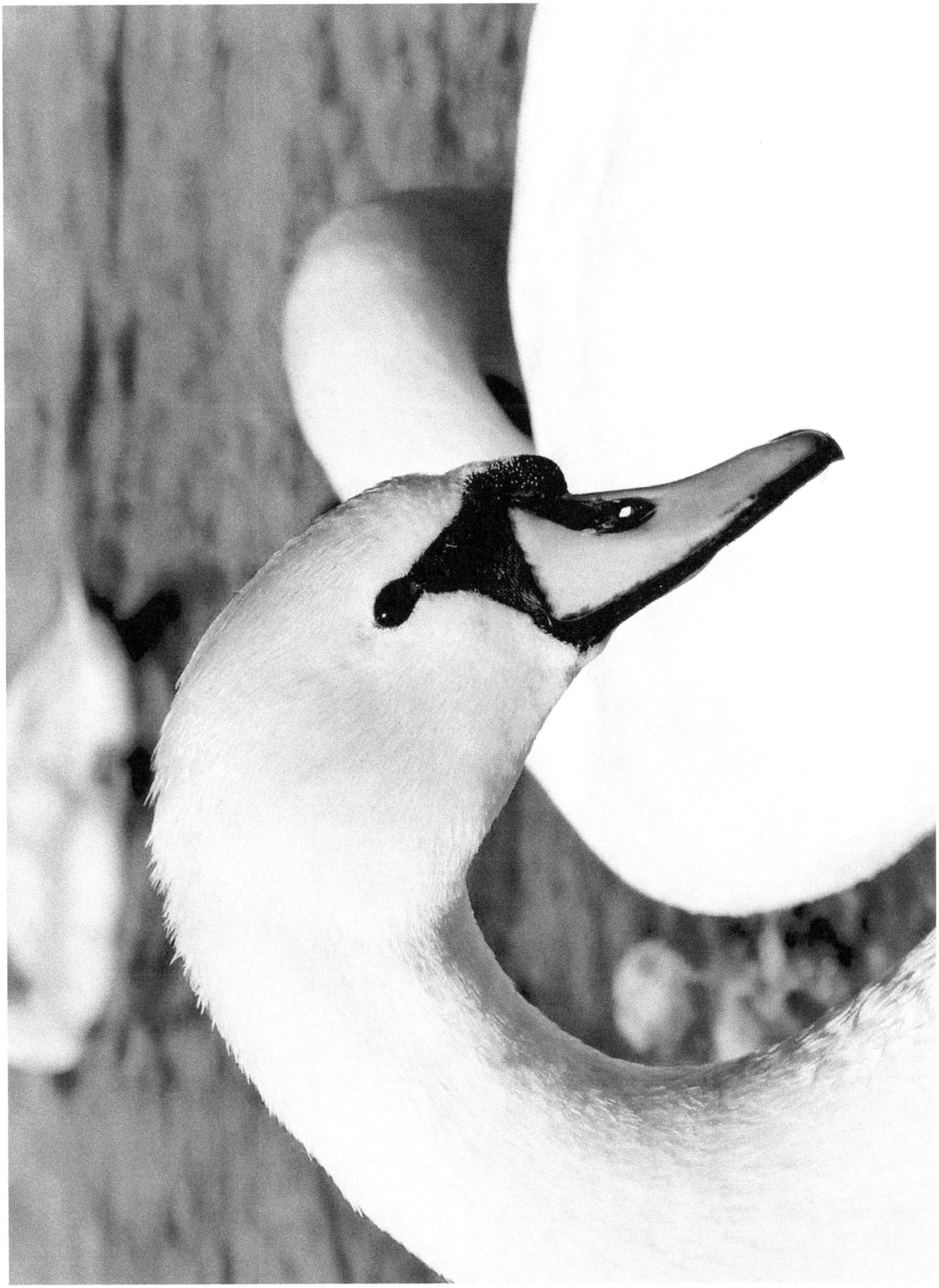

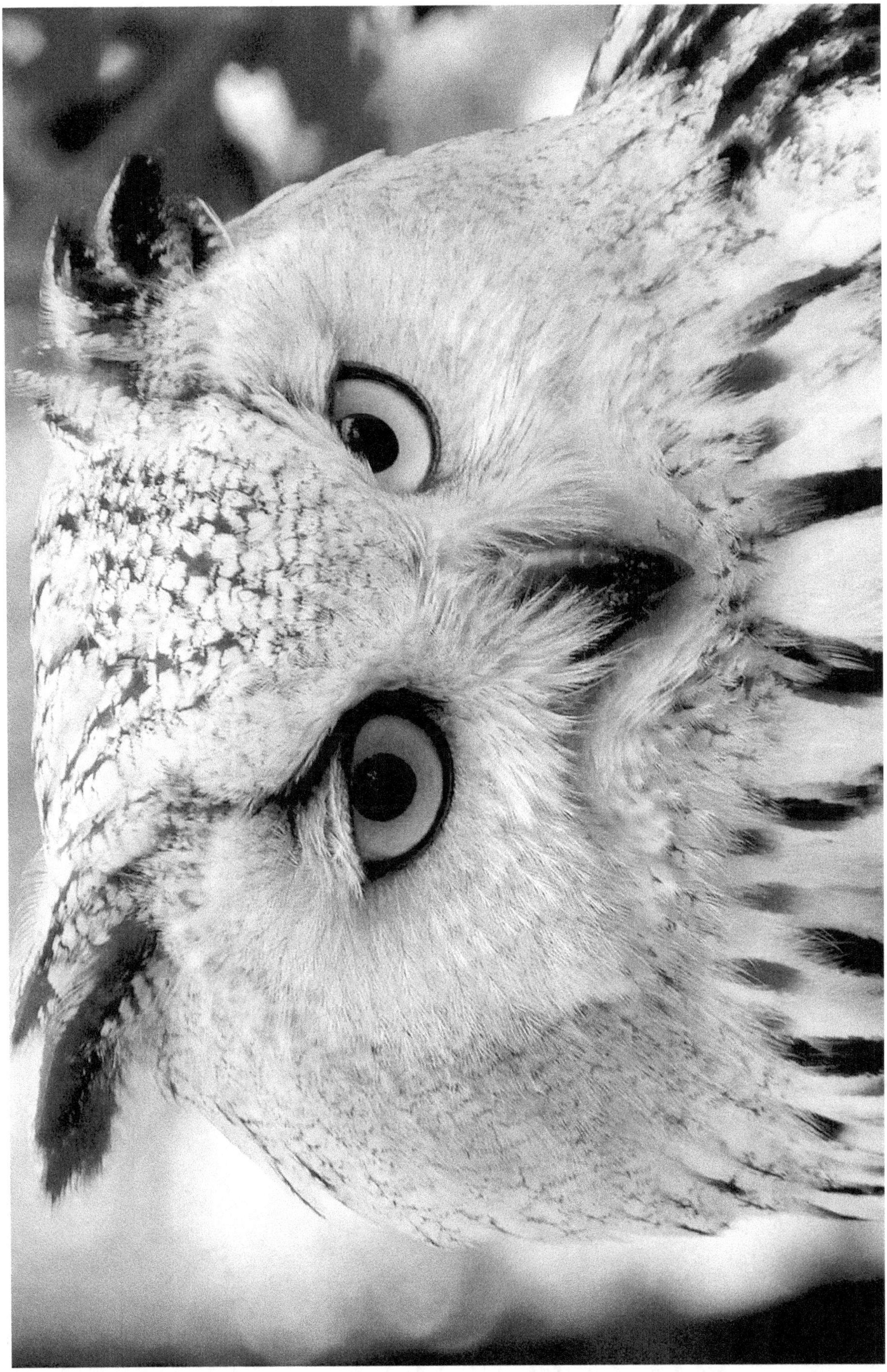

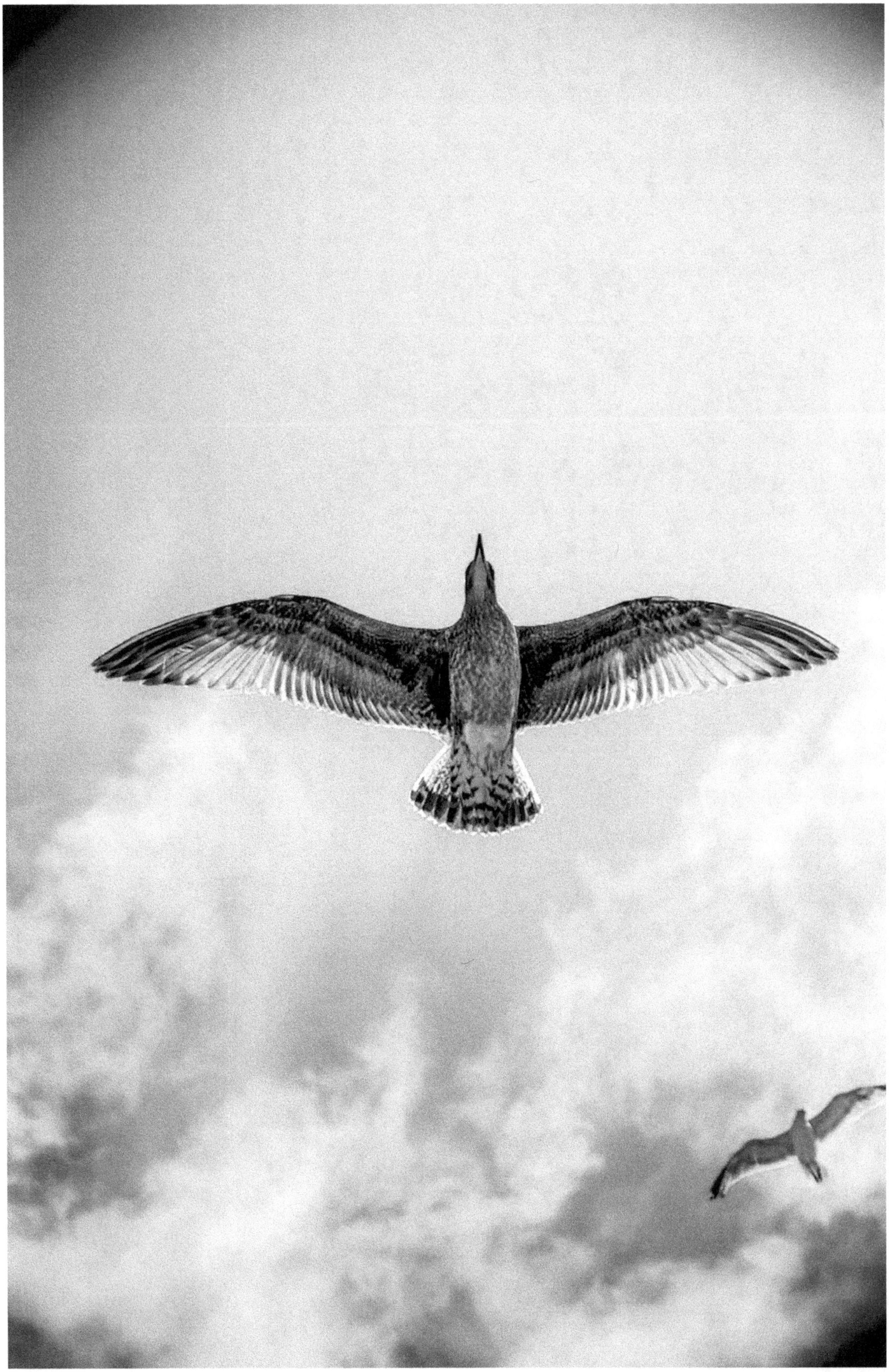

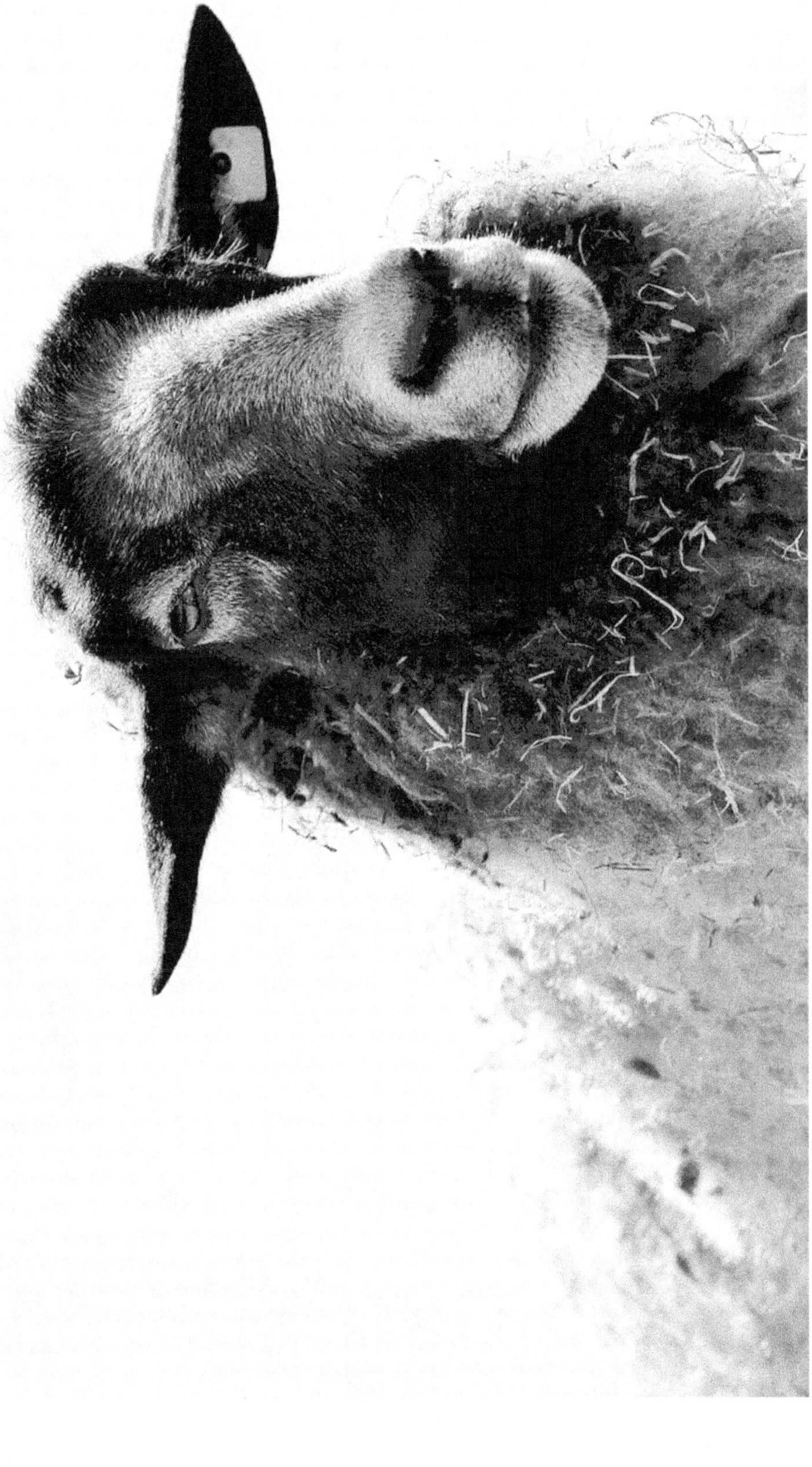

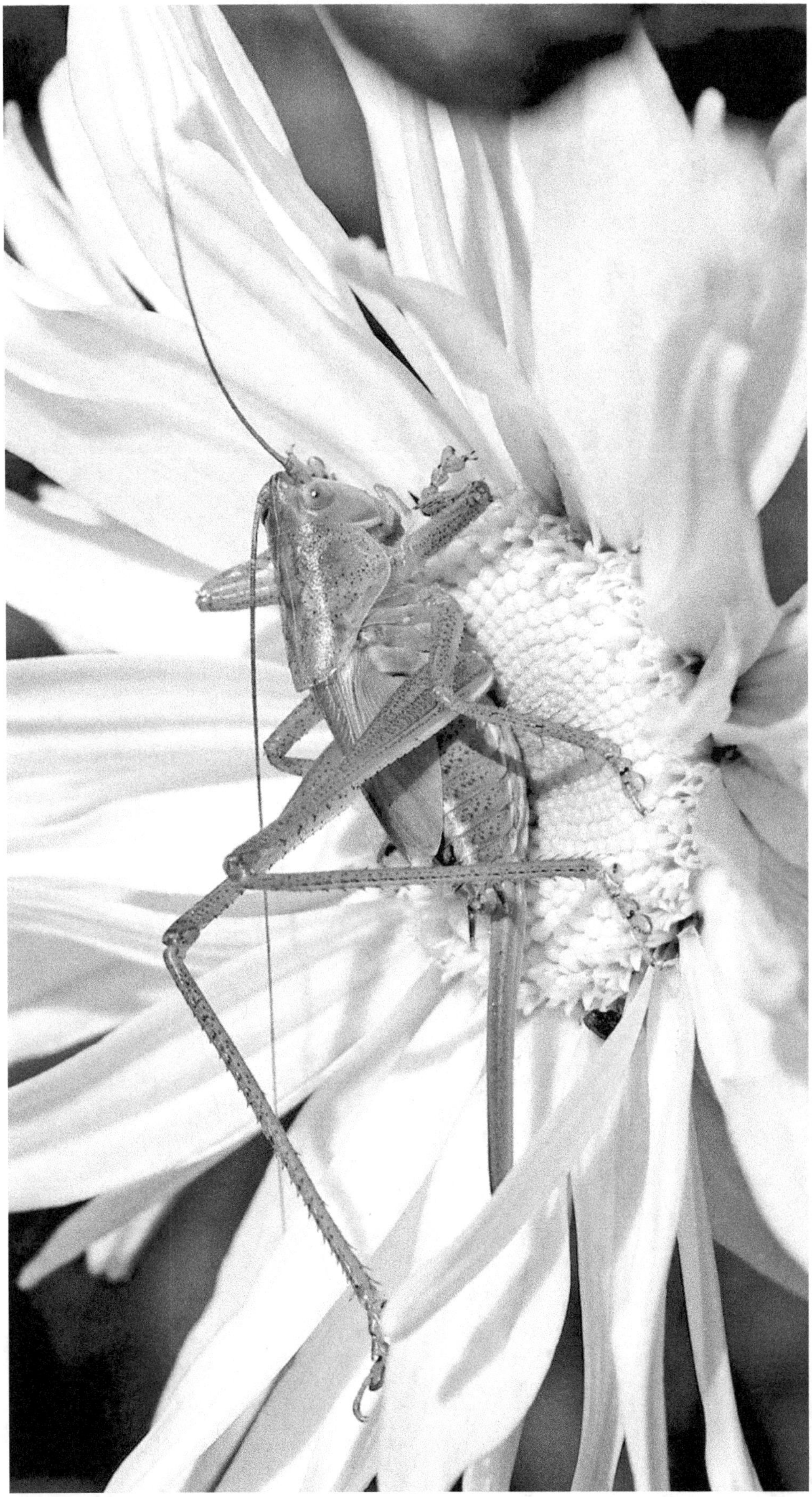

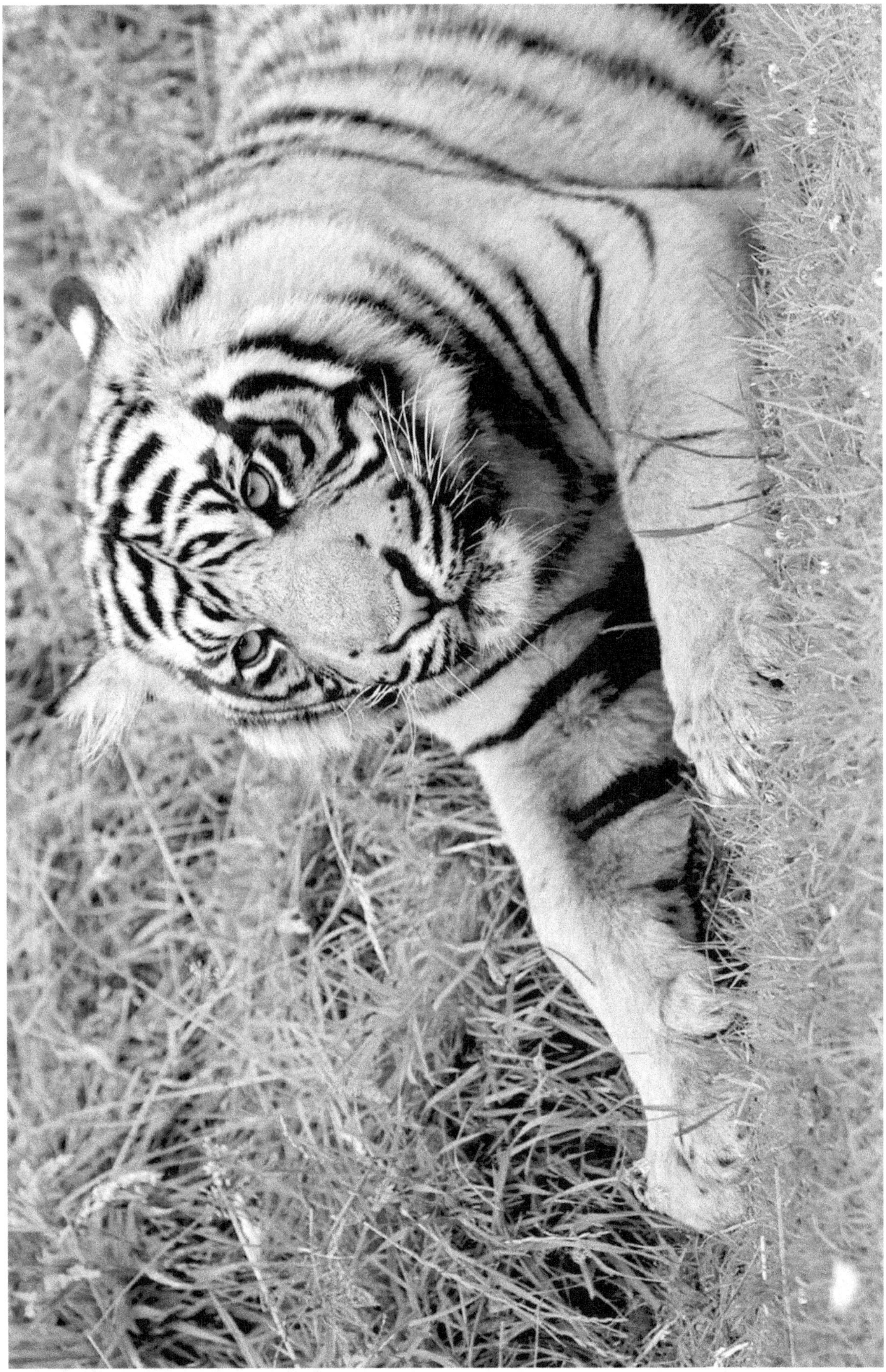

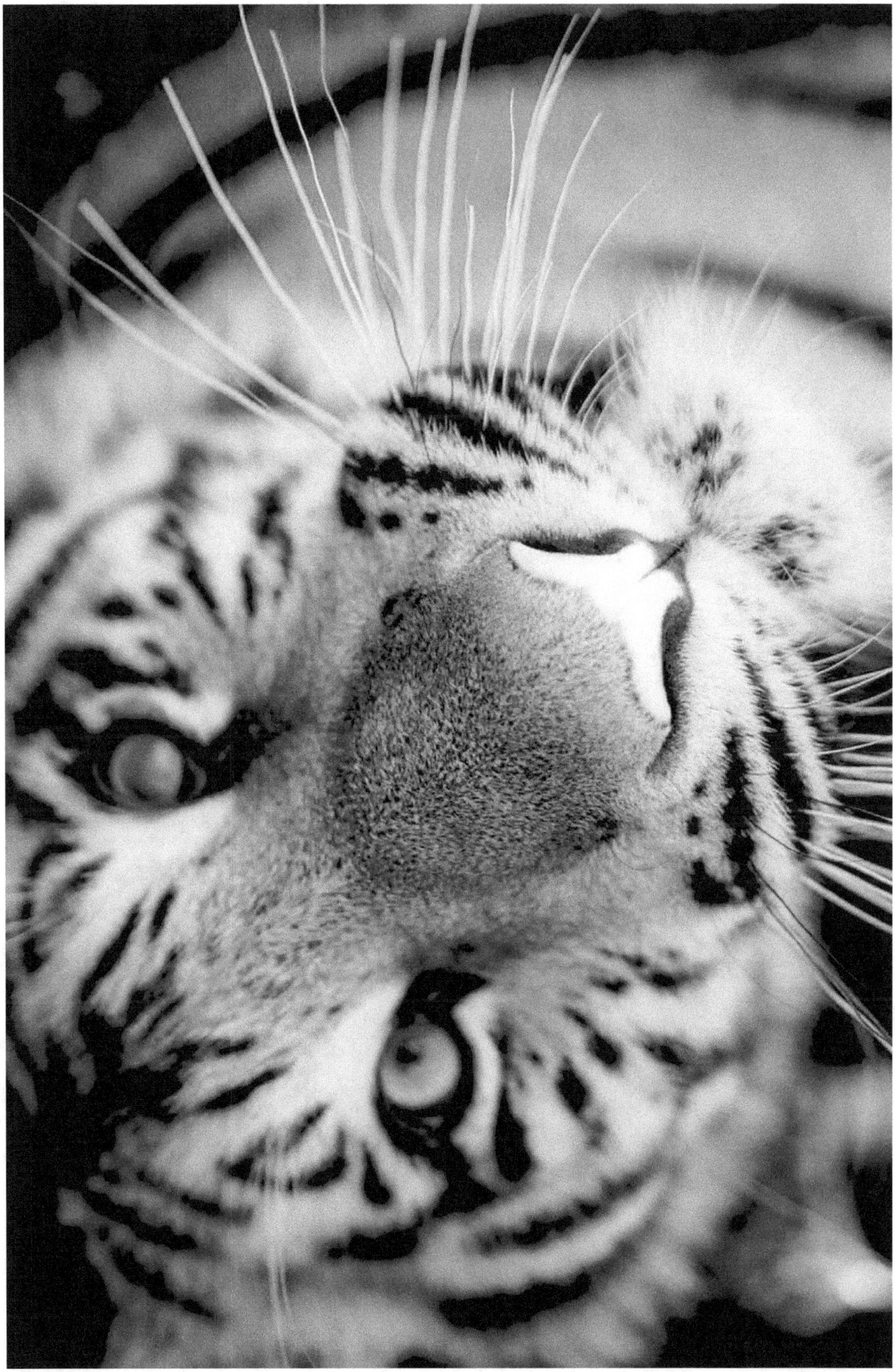